Vincent the Vixen

Sydni and Cricket

First published in 2018
by Jessica Kingsley Publishers
73 Collier Street
London N1 9BE, UK
and
400 Market Street, Suite 400
Philadelphia, PA 19106, USA

www.jkp.com

Copyright © Alice Reeves and Phoebe Kirk 2018

Library of Congress Cataloging in Publication Data
A CIP catalog record for this book is available from the Library of Congress

British Library Cataloguing in Publication Data
A CIP catalogue record for this book is available from the British Library

ISBN 978 1 78592 450 7
eISBN 978 1 78450 826 5

Printed and bound in China

Vincent the Vixen

A Story to Help Children Learn about Gender Identity

ALICE REEVES

Illustrated by
PHOEBE KIRK

Part of the  series

Jessica Kingsley Publishers
London and Philadelphia

Vincent the Fox loved playing
with his brothers and sisters.

Sometimes the fox cubs played
hide and seek in the woods.

Sometimes they all went
swimming in the stream.

Sometimes they played tricks
on the farmer's grumpy old cat.
Whatever the fox cubs did together,
they always had lots of fun.

When Mum and Dad needed peace and quiet, the fox cubs went to Betty the Badger's house to play.

They loved running around the winding tunnels, but the best thing about Betty's house was the dressing-up box full of her old clothes.

The fox cubs laughed at the old-fashioned dresses, draped themselves in the jewellery, and wobbled around in the high-heeled shoes.

Vincent loved dressing up more than anything in the world, because he could use his imagination to be anything he wanted to be.

Sometimes he was a rich queen sitting on the throne, watching over the whole kingdom.

Sometimes he was an evil witch
making potions out of snails, slugs,
bugs, and other slimy things.

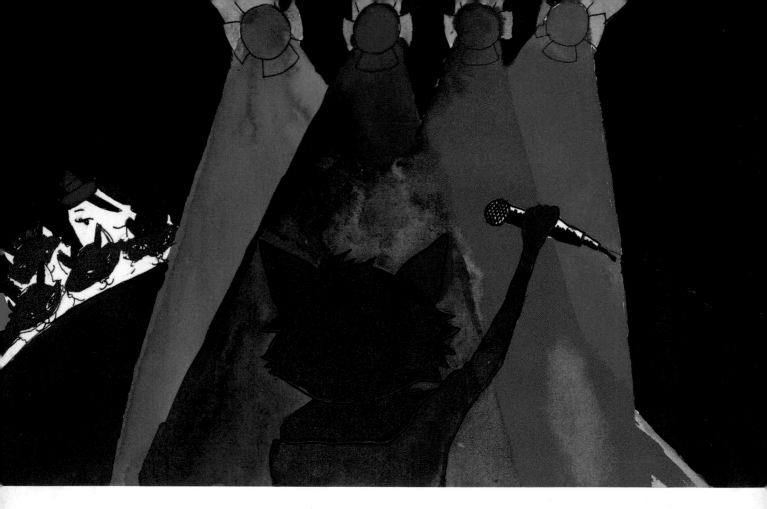

Sometimes he was a famous performer,
delighting crowds of adoring fans.

One day, Vincent's brothers and sisters asked him, "Vincent, why do you always pretend to be girls when we play dress up?"

Vincent didn't know what to say. He had never really thought about it before.

Suddenly, he didn't feel like playing.

He took off his dress and shoes and wandered through the tunnels until he found a quiet place to think.

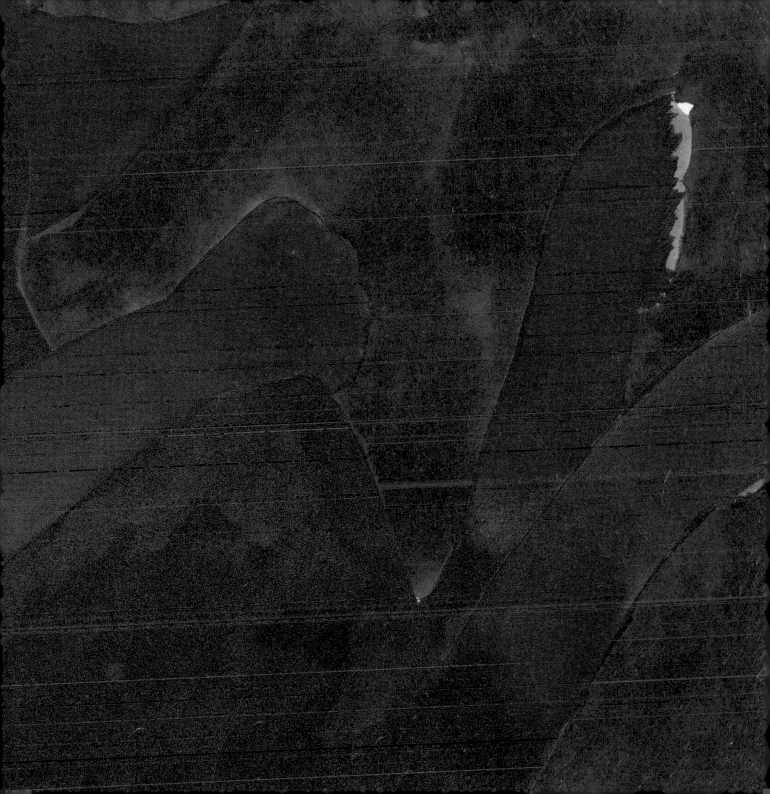

Vincent wondered whether he might be different from his brothers and sisters.

The fox cubs enjoyed doing lots of things together, but his brothers seemed happy being boys and his sisters seemed happy being girls.

When they played dress up, Vincent felt happiest when he wore beautiful dresses.

When they played make-believe, Vincent loved being queens and witches.

When he was just being Vincent, he wished he could be more like his sisters.

When Vincent went to bed that
night, he stayed awake for a long
time thinking about what his brothers
and sisters had asked him.

When he finally fell asleep, he dreamt of the dressing-up box and all the possibilities it held.

The next day, when Vincent was on his way home from school, he spotted Betty the Badger picking fruit for her dinner.

"Hello Vincent," said Betty. "You seemed quite sad yesterday, which isn't like you at all. What was the matter?"

"Oh, it's nothing," replied Vincent. He didn't think he could explain the way he was feeling.

"Was it something your brothers and sisters said that made you sad?" asked Betty. "Usually you all play so happily together when you visit my house!"

"Yes," said Vincent. "They asked why I always want to be girl characters when we play dress up."

Betty smiled. "Why does that matter, Vincent?" she asked.

Vincent took a deep breath and said, "It's because I think I'm really a girl."

Betty nodded. "In that case, I have a story that might help you," she said.

"When I was a young badger I loved playing make-believe with my sisters, just like you. I was also a boy badger, just like you.

"I started to think that maybe I was really a girl badger. The thoughts didn't go away, so I told my sisters how I was feeling.

"At first they were confused because they didn't understand, but they all listened patiently while I explained.

"From that day on
I've been called
Betty the Badger,
and I've been
happy ever since."

After listening to Betty's story, Vincent felt a lot less sad. "Thank you, Betty," he said.

He skipped all the way home, thinking about Betty's story. He was still smiling at dinner time.

"You seem very happy today,
Vincent!" said his mum.

"I am happy," replied Vincent.
"It's because I know who I am now."

"What wonderful news!" exclaimed Vincent's dad. "But what do you mean?"

"Everyone knows I love dressing up and playing make-believe," said Vincent, "but I'm really a girl fox, even when I'm not playing make-believe."

At first Vincent's parents were
puzzled, but the more they listened
to Vincent talk about his feelings,
the more they understood.

From that day on, instead of being a boy fox, Vincent grew up and they lived happily as Vincent the Vixen.

Notes for Teachers and Parents

The following open questions can be asked to inspire discussion.

Circle time before reading

★ What does the word "embarrassed" mean?

★ What does the word "proud" mean?

★ Share an interesting fact that people may not know about you that makes you feel proud.

★ How would it feel if this fact felt embarrassing instead of making you feel happy? Explain that for some people this is something that happens.

Mid-reading questions

These questions can be raised midway through the story, when Vincent is asked why they always dress up as girls.

★ Did Vincent's brothers and sisters say anything unkind?

★ Talk about the difference between asking questions and being unkind.

After reading

★ What is interesting and special about Vincent the Vixen?

★ Why does Vincent feel embarrassed at first?

★ How does Betty the Badger help Vincent feel proud of who they are?

★ Why is it so important to always feel proud of yourself?

★ What advice would you give to Vincent?

★ What would you say to Vincent's brothers and sisters?

Resources

Stonewall provides courses for teachers in
creating a trans-inclusive primary school:
www.stonewall.org.uk/get-involved/get-involved-
education/creating-trans-inclusive-school-primary

Mermaids supports gender diverse children and young
people up to 20 years old, and their families:
www.mermaidsuk.org.uk

More books to read

Who Are You? The Kid's Guide to Gender Identity by Brooke Pessin-Whedbee, illustrated by Naomi Bardoff.

Are You a Boy or Are You a Girl? by Sarah Savage and Fox Fisher, illustrated by Fox Fisher.

Acknowledgements

Thank you to everyone who helped us to tell Vincent's story, especially Matt from Stonewall and Elly, Aimee, and Maeve, for your constructive feedback, essential critique, and kind words.

It's important to note that Vincent's experience is just one fox's story
of the exploration and expression of their gender identity.

Also in the *Truth & Tails* series

Carlos the Chameleon
A Story to Help Empower Children to Be Themselves

As a chameleon, it's in Carlos's nature to change his colours in order to fit into his surroundings. Carlos is usually green, but can turn pink to join the flamingos, blue to match the frogs, and spotty to resemble the jaguars.

When the other animals find out that Carlos has been changing his colours in order to fit in, they reassure him that his own colour is beautiful and that he doesn't need to change who he is to be accepted and loved by his friends.

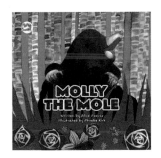

Molly the Mole
A Story to Help Children Build Self-Esteem
Molly is a mole with many friends, including a deer, a butterfly, and an owl. Sometimes Molly feels sad because she doesn't look the same as her friends, and feels very different to them. By helping each of them out with a task, Molly learns that her friends love her for the amazing qualities that are unique just to her.

Molly the Mole addresses the difference between the way we perceive ourselves and the way our friends and family perceive us. Molly learns the importance of being kind and patient with others, and that everyone is special in their own way.

Roxy the Raccoon
A Story to Help Children Learn about Disability and Inclusion
Roxy lives in the forest with her three best friends, who she loves to visit and play games with. Roxy is in a wheelchair, so sometimes it is harder for her to go to the same places and play the same games as the other animals.

Roxy and her friends realise that by making a few small changes and working together, they can make the forest a better place for everyone. Roxy teaches us that there are plenty of ways to be more inclusive of those who have a disability so that everyone can join in.